DIVING DEEP INTO YOUR HEALTH

How to *Live in Optimal Wellness*

DIVING DEEP INTO YOUR HEALTH

How to *Live in Optimal Wellness*

Kevin P. Greene, MD

YouSpeakIt
PUBLISHING
The Easy Way
to Get Your Book
Done Right ™

www.YouSpeakItPublishing.com

ISBN: 978-1-945446-52-8

To my wife, Janice: When I was lost on my own journey, you never made me feel alone. You are my strength, my defender, my refuge in the storm. Thank you from the bottom of my grateful heart for your unconditional love. I love you more than you will ever know.

Acknowledgments

To my boys, Tyler, Ryan, and Kyle: You are my world and my inspiration for everything I do in this life. I am so proud of the incredible young men you have become. Being your dad is the greatest gift I have ever received.

To my sister Cathleen, or *Dasheen,* as I called you so long ago: You have loved me, spoiled me, supported me, held me, cried with me, and protected me since the day I was born. I am forever grateful to have you watching over me.

And to my mom, Shirley Greene: I do not believe any written words can ever do justice to properly honor you. How do you put in a few sentences the impact you have had on my life? I will certainly try, but I hope and pray that my journey is testament enough to make you as proud of me as I am of you. Mom, of all the titles I have, the one I hold closest to my heart is *mama's boy.* You chose the thankless job of *Mom* over RN and even MD. Thank you, Mom, for your endless sacrifices, life lessons, hugs, kisses, and love. You are always with me, and this book is as much yours as it is mine.

Contents

Introduction

This book is a message of hope for all those whom traditional medicine has failed.

I wrote this book to carry the torch that my mom first lit in her own desperate search for answers, to honor her courage and determination in doing so, and to thank her for always putting her children first before all her pain. She is my role model, my hero, and my mom. I am my mother's son, and this book is the first step of my new journey.

My Journey, My Purpose

Kevin P. Greene, MD:

- Yale University, 1990, Bachelor of Arts in Chemical Engineering
- Georgetown University School of Medicine, 1995, MD
- University of Connecticut Internal Medicine Residency Program, Intern of the Year, 1996
- *Best Doctor of Southington,* 2002

My bio, my degrees, my awards. Do they really tell you *who* I am? If you have found my webpage or bought this book, then you are looking for help. You are searching for an answer to make you feel better so you can embrace and enjoy your incredible gift of life. You are looking for that doctor you can trust to truly invest their time into your health and well-being. You cannot find that doctor from a stat sheet. Don't get me wrong; I worked incredibly hard to earn all my degrees, and I'm very proud of them. But my degrees and achievements don't tell you who I really am.

> *. . . to know even one life has breathed easier*
> *because you have lived.*
> *This is to have succeeded.*
> ~ often attributed to Emerson

I was born February 13, 1968, in Waterbury, Connecticut. My parents named me *Michelle* until they found out that their youngest of four children was a boy. My mom is Shirley Greene, who readily gave up her RN to be *Mom* to Jack, Nick, Cathleen, and me. She is 100 percent Italian and grew up on a farm in Oakville, Connecticut. She ended up in the operating rooms and emergency rooms of St. Mary's Hospital in Waterbury, Connecticut. She was brilliant at her job and was offered a full scholarship to attend medical school. This was an incredible opportunity for a woman in 1959, but she was pregnant with my brother Jack and knew her true calling was to be our mom.

My dad is Jack Greene, the oldest of five Irish brothers born and raised in the projects of Waterbury,

Connecticut. He joined the Marines and then spent the rest of his career at Northeast Utilities, where he never missed one day of work for over forty-five years.

I am proud to say I grew up a *mama's boy*. My mom was my world growing up. I never left her side. My sister Cathleen spoiled me as much as my mom and continues to this day. We lived in Wolcott, Connecticut, a small cow town filled with the most amazing people in the world. It was an incredible childhood.

As I grew older, my mom would tell me stories of her life as a nurse. She would laugh out loud recalling some of her favorite patients she cared for. She would tell me about all the doctors that she worked with and described the hospital operating and emergency rooms in full detail to me. She loved being a nurse, and I loved hearing all her stories.

After traditional medicine failed her as a young woman, she decided to take her health into her own hands. She taught herself about insulin and sugar, herbs, supplements, gut inflammation, and the immune system, to name just a few. She amassed an entire library of medical books, all tattered with the pages worn out from her constant reading and referencing. She was a true naturopath, homeopath, functional medicine doctor, endocrinologist, psychiatrist—a true multi-specialist—just no degrees to hang on her wall.

She was constantly teaching all of us how to live healthier, more productive lives. This was the environment I was raised in. She taught all of us the importance of education. She cracked the whip for us to study while my dad showed us the importance of a hard day's work.

There was no need for my dad to teach me a good work ethic, he simply led by example. Working for Northeast Utilities, he would go for days and weeks during snowstorms and hurricanes to restore power. He never complained, just worked. When he was undergoing chemotherapy to cure his kidney disease, he was treated in the morning and then went to work with his nausea in the afternoon. He never missed a day at work, but most importantly he never missed a football, baseball, or basketball game of mine either. I truly had the best of both worlds with two incredible role models.

If you are going to entrust me with your health, you need to know whom you are hiring for the job. My incredible childhood and family environment created a desire and determination in me at a young age. I not only excelled in the classroom but on the baseball and football fields as well. I was driven to succeed in all aspects of my young life. I never received lower than an A throughout elementary, middle school, and high school, while being voted MVP my senior year for both football and baseball. From the halls of my beloved Wolcott High School, I was the first and only student to be accepted to Yale University. I played baseball and graduated with a chemical engineering degree. But thanks to my mom, medicine was always my passion.

"Are you sure, Kevin? Because medicine is the jealous lover!"

This was my mom's first reaction and warning when I was accepted to Georgetown University School of Medicine. I was too young to fully realize what she meant, but I now know exactly what she was telling me.

My best friend since age sixteen is Janice. I have five best days of my life: the first one was the day that I married her, my high school sweetheart, in 1995. The others were when I became a dad to my three beautiful sons: Tyler, Ryan, and Kyle.

Janice and I would dream about what our kids would look like and how our family life would be. But we did not anticipate the demands of my other love, medicine—as my mom had warned me.

Every third or fourth night during my residency training, I worked a thirty-six-hour shift, which was vital to my education to become the physician that I am today. But that also meant every third or fourth night,

Janice was home alone. When residency was over and I finally started a practice on my own, the work hours got even worse. My thirty-six-hour shifts every three days were exchanged for fourteen-hour shifts *every day.*

But Janice was no longer home alone, she was with our newborn sons. Never once did she complain about the seemingly endless hours alone raising our three boys. She embraced being Tyler, Ryan, and Kyle's mommy. She never saw it as a sacrifice during those earlier years, but a privilege to be their mom. She assured me that she would take care of home and our growing family, while I took care of work. She has never left my side through it all. She is my rock.

There was a time in my recent life when I was lost. My personal life's journey took a detour, filled with doubt, disbelief, and indescribable pain. My fairy-tale marriage ended in the second-floor courtroom in New Britain, Connecticut. I lost my way and almost lost my family. But it was during my time of solitude and at my lowest point, when I was lifted back up by the unconditional love of Janice, Tyler, Ryan, and Kyle. My lonely, dark days were then gradually replaced with self-discovery, faith, forgiveness, and rebirth.

> *Life takes us to unexpected places,*
> *love brings us home.*
>
> ~ Author unknown

So, I'm sure your wondering about the fifth best day in my life. With our three beautiful sons standing by my side, Janice and I remarried on December 27, 2017.

With God by our side, we have a much deeper understanding and appreciation of each other. She inspires me every day to be a better man, husband, father, and doctor. She is my beacon of light in the stormiest of weather. Listening to the words of Pastor Ron at Faith Living Church across the street from my office, I choose every day to live in a world of gratitude. I am forever grateful for Janice. She has taught me the true meaning of sacrifice and unconditional love.

Knowledge Is Power

The field of medicine changes on a daily, if not hourly, basis. My mom instilled in me my thirst for learning. My quest for knowledge began in first grade at Lewis School with my favorite teacher, Karen Mathews, and it continues today. Being a physician comes with many responsibilities; the most important is remaining a student and constantly educating oneself. It is what my patients deserve.

It started with board certification in my field of internal medicine and continues with remaining on the cutting-edge of medicine. This requires even more sacrifice of time away from my family and a commitment to excellence in my profession. I readily accept this responsibility because it is who I am.

> *The inferior doctor treats actual sickness;*
> *the mediocre doctor attends to impending sickness;*
> *the superior doctor prevents sickness.*
> ~ Chinese Proverb

Health Optimization Medicine

My approach is to combine the best of all evidence-based medicine to give you a wider range of choices. My health optimization approach embodies elements from traditional, integrative, functional, and age-management medicine and employs them in a preventive, proactive way to meet your specific age-related issues, medical challenges, optimal health needs, and more. My goal for every patient is not just to prevent diseases, but to achieve optimal wellness.

> *Listen to your patients and you will have*
> *the diagnosis 95 percent of the time.*
> ~ Shirley A. Greene, RN

Of all the advice my mom has given me throughout my life, this wisdom was the best. It seems like such a simple concept to engage in a conversation with another person and truly listen to what they are saying. In my opinion, this is not a skill that needs to be taught in lectures and in the classroom. Engaging in a conversation and listening to the patient comes from within. It comes naturally to me, and it is vital to forming the doctor-patient bond that is like no other. It is crucial to listen to properly do my job. As my patient, you need to be heard. I will be listening.

Have you heard this saying? *Do what you love, and love what you do – and you will never work a day in your life.*

I love my job. It is really that simple. This passion for medicine began at a very young age as I listened to so many wonderful stories from my mom. Seeing the look of pride on her face, the joy in her smile, and hearing her laughter as she described her other life as a nurse showed me that it was not just a job for her, but a calling. Surrounded by my mom's loving guidance, I began my own journey. Becoming a doctor was never a choice for me. It has always been my purpose. It is a privilege and honor to care for the thousands of patients who bless me with their trust.

I choose to live in a world of gratitude, and I am forever grateful to my beloved patients as well, who allow me to live my dream.

So, let me help you in your journey to an optimal life. Allow me to join in your fight. I look so forward to meeting you.

My Real Biography

- Son/Brother: 1968
- MD: 1995
- Husband: 1995
- Dad: 1997 Tyler, 2000 Ryan, 2002 Kyle, 2007 Eli, our four-legged son
- Coach: McCabe Waters Little League Champions, Bristol, Connecticut, 2014
- Husband: 2017!
- Student of medicine: *Always!*

As you're reading the book, I'd like you to view this as a conversation between two friends. This book tells my story, so reading it from beginning to end, sequentially, is highly recommended.

Know that you are not alone. Know that I have now joined you in this fight to regain your health, every step of the way.

See you soon!

Dr. Kevin Greene

CHAPTER ONE

Being Proactive
Instead of Reactive

The inferior doctor treats actual sickness;
the mediocre doctor attends to impending sickness;
the superior doctor prevents sickness.
~ Chinese Proverb

IF THERE IS A PROBLEM BREWING,
I WILL FIND IT

Medicine today doesn't allow the primary care provider enough time to see problems on the horizon. The patients feel sick, they come in, and they get treated; but that's not what medicine is all about. Medicine is about finding a problem that's brewing and then trying to fix it *before* it develops. Hence, I would rather be proactive than reactive. I will treat the problem when it arises, but my goal is to have found the conditions that might bring about a problem before it ever arises.

Taking Advantage of Science

When I became a physician, it required me to become a constant student. What I learned twenty years ago in medical school may or may not apply to what is happening now in today's scientific world. My goal is to stay on the cutting edge of medicine, as well as treatment.

In order to do that, I never stop learning. I go to continuing medical education classes to learn what the issues are, how to discover them, and how to treat them. This takes effort — time from my family, from my office, from my work — but it is essential to stay on top of advancements in medicine, and to treat each patient in the way they want to be treated.

It requires being a forever student and making sure what I'm discovering is backed by science and is evidence-based. This is my obligation to my patients, it is my obligation to the medical degree that I worked hard to obtain, and it is my obligation to the Hippocratic oath that I took when I became a physician.

Part of my training is to remain board certified in my specialty, Internal Medicine. Again, this requires time away from work and time away from family. It requires effort to keep learning, and to always be on top of the science. In addition to doing what is necessary to retain my board certification, I regularly attend lectures, read the most up-to-date scientific articles, and then learn how to apply that information to my practice, which I can then pass onto my patients.

Finding the problem is the easy part. Trying to figure out how to treat it, and then how to prevent it from ever coming back, is the challenge.

Green Is Good

It's important for me as a physician to ensure that my patients clearly understand the results that I'm telling them, and that they take this knowledge home with them. Often, patients are only absorbing a third of the information that their physician is trying to convey to them.

I have been accused of repeating myself — perhaps from my Italian background. I talk with my hands, and I tend to repeat important points, but it's for a reason. It's because I want my patients to clearly understand exactly what we are discussing, so they can clearly understand that we need to do something about it.

One advanced testing that I do is Boston Heart Diagnostics laboratory work, which is advanced cardiovascular and lipid testing.

There are many reasons why I love this particular company's lab work, but one of the main reasons is that their results are color-coded:

- Green = normal
- Yellow = not normal
- Red = bad

This is crucial for my patients to know, so they understand what our goal is when we re-check the labs. The lab work also tells patients where the problems are and how we need to address them. I want patients to walk away from a visit with me knowing exactly what we found and what we can do about it.

Unfortunately, in today's medical world, the doctor has only a very short time to spend with each patient. This is, by far, nowhere near the amount of time needed to report the results and to make sure that the patient understands those results.

This shift in medicine over the past twenty years is one of my biggest frustrations. One of my greatest mentors, Dr. John Polio, took the time to talk to patients, hold their hands, and ask them if they had any questions. He was not on a time limit; or, if he was, the patient had no idea. He is one of many examples of true doctors that I have had the pleasure of training under.

With this approach, I am proud to say that I work with some of the most educated patients because I take the time to explain:

- The tests we're doing
- Why we're doing them
- The results of the tests
- What we're going to do about any issues

When I say *green is good, and yellow and red are bad,* that sets the bar with my patients and provides us with a target to attain: we are going to be proactive and change those colors to green. Any issue that initially tested in the yellow range will never go to red, and reds and yellows will eventually become green. This is being proactive instead of being reactive.

I do not want to wait until a disaster happens. The tests that I perform allow me to see potential problems before they actually happen. My patients fully understand what needs to be done, and they have evidence of their progress on their follow-up visits.

Fail to Plan, Plan to Fail

The most important mentor in my life, with regards to my profession and life in general, is my mom. Her name is Shirley A. Greene, and she is a nurse. She spent most of her profession in the emergency room and the operating rooms of St. Mary's Hospital in Waterbury, Connecticut. One of the many things she taught me was: *Fail to plan, plan to fail.* This applied to many aspects of my life, whether it was preparing for a baseball game, for a big test, or any other important event in my life.

I've adopted this saying in my approach medicine, and I repeat this mantra to my patients. I then work with them to plan a road map for what we need to do, and a course of action for treatment. I tell them that if we don't plan this, then we will fail. I share with them the importance of creating this road map together because it will guide them through the next months or years. Most importantly, I help them understand that the road map will get them to their goal of optimal health, wellness, and overall quality of life.

Too many of my colleagues are too tired or too busy to take the time to see the signs that are present for their own patients. Unfortunately, these patients suffer a huge disservice. I never want to be that doctor.

One of my favorite sayings is: *I cannot prevent what I cannot predict.* For that reason, I am always searching for the best diagnostic test currently available. I am constantly reaching beyond the *standard of care* to offer the best treatment plans. Searching for these diagnostic tests requires time and effort, and my patients benefit greatly from this extra work.

I was once called an outlier by the medical director of Connecticare insurance company for being the only primary care provider ordering Boston Heart Diagnostic lab work. I have been called a lot of names in my career, but never an outlier.

My response was, "Did you ever consider my approach as the new standard of care, and all the other doctors being the outliers?" I was being reprimanded for doing my job—utilizing the best tools and diagnostics to prevent heart disease, the number-one killer in both men and women in the USA.

My solution was to have the entire ten board members I was sitting in front of—yes, ten in total, all for me—to get a Boston Heart lab test on themselves. It is then that they would all see how superior this particular advanced lab work was over the standard-of-care labs that all the other obedient providers were ordering. Their response was to drop me from their panel if I kept ordering the lab tests. I simply could not let my Connecticare patients down. I found other ways continue to diagnose and treat them per my superior standards of care without getting thrown out of Connecticare. Dr. Kevin Greene, The Outlier: I like how that sounds, like a John Wayne character.

It is crucial, in the profession that I chose, to be a constant student. My patients deserve that, and they have put their trust in me to take care of them.

GO TO THE GREEN

It's important for you to set goals for your personal health, but in order for you to achieve those goals, you need to have a system in place, or you will likely fail. You need a coach as well as a doctor. The *green* refers to lab results in the normal range; they are the targets that the personalized system I create for you is designed to attain.

Red Flags Paint a Picture

When the results are in from the tests that I choose to order — based on the history and the physical exam — there will ultimately be red flags on the test results. The solution is not simply looking at one test result and trying to fix that one problem in particular. I look at the whole picture. I look at all the red flags that I have found within the lab results. These results then paint a picture for me of how your body is operating right now. The results show me your current health and the potential problems you're heading toward if no changes are made.

It's my obligation to paint the picture for patients of their current health, whether or not it's a pretty picture; in most cases, it's not. I don't pull any punches because I'm talking about one of the most important aspects of a person's life — health. It's essential to be as truthful as

I can in order for patients to understand the gravity of the situation.

And it is not just you that I am affecting. If I keep you healthy, then your family and everyone who depends on you benefits as well.

In order to paint an accurate picture for my patients, they need to have all the essential information. To do that, I need to take advantage of the science that's currently available. Each patient's picture is unique, and it is my job to create a targeted, individualized treatment plan for each of them.

It's Not Just the Number

Going back to the Boston Heart Diagnostic laboratory values, in my experience, many patients are focused on the number itself; for example, the total cholesterol.

"What's my bad cholesterol, Doc?"

To give the patient the number of their *bad* cholesterol is again doing them a disservice. The results indicate more than just a number, they also point to the size and shape of cholesterol. This is just one of the many examples of needing to dig a little deeper when interpreting one of these test results; I need to see *why* that result is abnormal.

When I'm training students, I always tell them to ask *why* until they have an answer that satisfies them.

I ask the following questions:

- Why is this patient sick?
- Why isn't that treatment working?
- Why is this treatment working, but not resolving the issue?

I encourage my students, physician assistants, and nurse practitioners who work with me to ask the question: *Why?* until the question is answered satisfactorily. I teach them to keep digging under the surface until the reason for this abnormality is found.

It's satisfying when a patient asks me why the other docs didn't check this type of test and just used the standardized testing.

I answer them as honestly as I can, saying that I cannot speak for other healthcare practitioners, but it's probably because they're not aware that this test is available.

This reiterates the philosophy that I need to keep digging under the surface to find the reason a patient's labs and their tests are abnormal. It's only when I dig deep and find the *true reason* that I can paint a picture and figure out a treatment plan that's going to work.

Each Treatment Has Its Own Role

A great example of this idea is vitamin supplements. Each vitamin targets a specific abnormality in the lab work that I check. They each have their own role, which has been scientifically proven to work.

However, when you take these supplements as a whole, they all contribute to treating another problem, for example, plaque in the carotid arteries. Red yeast rice will treat the bad cholesterol, fish oil will correct the fatty acid index, and niacin will treat the low HDL: they all contribute and have been proven to deal with plaque stabilization, as well as plaque regression.

Sharing this information illustrates to the patient the importance of remaining compliant with the treatment plan because each treatment has its own individual role, and, as a whole, plays a role in achieving optimal health, wellness, and longevity.

FORM THE TEAM AND CREATE A ROAD MAP

It takes teamwork to make a dream work! We have to form a team in order to tackle the problems that are found. I tell my patients not to fear the abnormalities because together we will tackle each one. I impress upon them the importance of tackling problems together. They also need to know that I'm the captain of the team and that my role is to guide them and to be available when they need me. That's the recipe for success.

We Are Working Together

Education and knowledge are power. With my patients, I am not only their doctor, I am their coach — the coach who teaches them what needs to be done in order to achieve optimal wellness. Like all the best teams, my beloved New York Yankees have won many World Series championships because players and the coaches are all working together.

That is the concept that I take into the exam room; we're forming a team where I guide patients through what needs to be done in order to achieve their goals.

We need to:

- Work together
- Keep the lines of communication open
- Tackle each problem as it occurs

This is the only way that we'll achieve the goal of optimal wellness.

I tell all my patients that it's a team effort, and that I will help them every step of the way.

Positive Mind Equals Positive Outcomes

The power of positive thinking has been proven many times over in the scientific world. Despite this, when I tell patients that we are going to make changes in many areas of their lives, this tends to depress some of them.

A successful approach to treatment includes making changes in:

- Lifestyle
- Diet
- Exercise regimen
- Supplements

I understand because I've been there as that patient. I've been overweight, I've had the bad cholesterol, I've been the former athlete that has let my health go, and I know sometimes it's much easier to just give up and just hope for the best. But that's not what we're all about.

We need to remain positive. Once we have that positive attitude and we know what we're trying to achieve, the obstacles in front of us suddenly disappear; there are only challenges that we will eventually overcome.

I've seen it time and time again with some of my beloved patients who have been diagnosed with cancer, yet have remained positive throughout their treatment course and absolutely sailed through their treatment to become cancer-free. The same applies for my patients who needed to lose weight and needed to change their entire lifestyle.

As long as you remain positive, there's really nothing that we can't handle together.

That's why I say that a positive mind equals a positive outcome. There's no need to be negative. Once a patient begins to see results, remaining positive throughout the course of treatment becomes easy.

Attitude determines altitude.

It's a Journey, Not a Race

For a lot of my patients, the problems that we find have developed over years. Therefore, it's going to take months, maybe even a year, to correct the problems. A realistic road map doesn't allow for any disappointment. There are going to be obstacles and challenges that we'll need to overcome together.

There will be periods when you'll get to your goal in a much faster time frame than we anticipated, but the key is that these are permanent lifestyle changes for this journey we call life. There's no race to get where you need to go because once you reach your health goals, you're going to maintain that optimal health for the rest of your life.

The journey may be shorter than you anticipate, but it may also be longer than you had hoped for. No matter what, it's a journey that's moving in a positive direction, creating a better future and a healthier outcome.

When you know that it's a journey, not a race, the pressures of achieving these goals and targets become less stressful. Maintaining optimal health and wellness is certainly a journey that has its ups and downs. But as long as you have me as your coach and your teammate, guiding you through all of this, then the ultimate goal will be achieved.

CHAPTER TWO

_____

Pay Attention

Listen to your patients,
and you'll get the diagnosis 95 percent of the time.
~ Shirley Greene, RN

TOO LITTLE TIME

A big reason for the healthcare crisis is the very little time that most doctors allot per visit. This is ultimately a doctor's choice — but not mine.

I Need Time to Do My Job

When you are putting your health in my hands, I need to know everything about you — your family history, your social history, your past — in order to determine a proper treatment plan. Because your health is important, this is something that cannot be rushed at all.

Being Italian and Irish, I need five minutes just to introduce myself to you. The extra time is going to allow us to build a relationship, first and foremost, so you can gain trust in me. You need to feel comfortable in telling me everything about you, your history, and your family, and that requires time.

Once that rapport is established, then we need the time to go into your personal history, and for you to tell me the story of your health journey. This crucial part of the history is something that cannot be rushed, and modern medicine has dictated to us that we need to do it in fifteen minutes or less. I refuse to accept that because I cannot do my job in fifteen minutes or less.

However Long It Takes

I have been in private practice for the last twenty years. One of the complaints I hear frequently from my patients is that I get behind, and they have to wait. My answer to them is simply that I was addressing the needs of the patient ahead of them. I also remind them that if they need me for the next thirty to forty-five minutes with their health concerns, then I will take the time necessary to do so thoroughly.

Unfortunately, this leaves many patients upset, in spite of my trying to stay on time, but I refuse to sacrifice good-quality medical care to stay on a schedule and keep all my patients happy and on time.

Primary care is a double-edged sword. As a practitioner, you have no idea what's coming through your door; it could be a simple case or a difficult case. The current healthcare system dictates that doctors need to stay on time, and we need to see a higher volume of patients in order to remain profitable. I refuse to accept that rule. If a patient needs me for any urgent or serious matter, I will be with them for however long it takes.

Tell Me Everything

Through my twenty years of experience, and with the help of the advanced testing that I now incorporate into my practice, I realize the importance of getting a complete history. A complete history does not just include your medications, your latest labs, and your surgeries in the last ten years; it also includes a detailed family history, as well as a detailed social history.

During this detailed history-taking, nuggets are discovered. We cannot underestimate the power of genetics. Whether you realize it or not, the illnesses and diseases that your parents, grandparents, and siblings have dealt with are very much an important part of your history as well. Your social history is just as important, including whether you drink alcohol, smoke cigarettes, or tried recreational drugs. Your work environment and social stressor should also be considered.

As an example of my detailed history-taking, one of my patients had been diagnosed with bipolar disorder at the age of thirty-five. In an educational class, I learned that even the mildest of concussions can interfere with the hypothalamus-pituitary axis, where most hormones — signals in your body — are created. The consequences of this disruption can come five to ten years later in the form of what appears to be a psychiatric disease.

I was taught that no patient is deficient in pharmaceutical medications, so when I dug deeper with this patient, I realized that in his twenties and thirties, he was very active in sports and had sustained a few mild concussions. That led me to check hormone levels and discover that the disruption in his twenties and thirties eventually led to the misdiagnosis of bipolar disorder in his forties.

If I had not asked him to tell me everything about his life, I never would have discovered his hormone imbalance. I addressed his issues with hormone replacement and stopped his bipolar medication.

Dr. Mark Gordon out of Los Angeles calls himself a *neuro-endocrinologist*. He's an unbelievable speaker, and he made the link. To bring this kind of knowledge back to my practice, and then actually use it to make a difference in someone's life, is powerful. We're detectives; I'll talk about that in the next section.

Dr. Gordon made the link between traumatic brain injury—even mild traumatic brain injury—and where the hypothalamus and the pituitary gland are located in the head. Any disorder to that axis, which is so sensitive, can actually lead to disruption in the hormones.

There are a variety of different signals, but he found that issues don't manifest immediately. Problems may appear decades later. Now, whenever I have a patient that was previously diagnosed with a psychiatric disorder, I look at their hormone levels, and I get a detailed history.

Dr. Gordon gave a great example in his lecture. He described how a doctor-friend called and said, "I checked. This guy has never hit his head."

Dr. Gordon responded, "Well, did you ask about his teenage years? No? Well, get him back and ask."

When the patient was asked, he responded that he hadn't suffered any head injuries in his teenage years. Dr. Gordon told his friend to keep digging. It turns out that this patient had fallen off a swing set when he was an adolescent. That led to the proper screening, which then led to replacing the medication he had been taking for the misdiagnosed psychiatric disorder. He got better.

Dr. Gordon also made this connection with soldiers. I can go on and on about him, and that's just one example.

Now when I take a history of my patients, it includes these questions:

- Have you ever had a traumatic brain injury?
- Have you ever been knocked out or lost consciousness?
- Have you ever had a concussion?

It's a hot topic now, particularly since the biographical sports drama movie *Concussion,* which exposes *chronic traumatic encephalopathy* in the National Football League.

In order for me to do my job properly — which is why you hired me — I need to have the time to get a proper history and a proper introduction with you. To do this in modern medicine is impossible for many practitioners, given the limitations imposed on them.

The insurance companies have dictated what they will pay, and how often they'll pay it. Doctors will go bankrupt if they attempt to spend more time than is allotted, but there are doctors, like many of my colleagues and me, who have broken free from the chains of the modern medicine platform, which allots us the proper amount of time to do our job.

I HEAR YOU

You, the patient, are frustrated with the current healthcare system. I hear you loud and clear. Your frustrations on your side are equaled by frustrations on the physician's side. We don't have to accept this. You need to find a physician like me who is going to break away from these chains and create an environment that's conducive to proper diagnosis and treatment, which then leads to optimal health and wellness.

Leave No Stone Unturned

My greatest mentor is my mom, who is a registered nurse. When I started practicing medicine, she said, "Truly listen to your patients, and they will give you the diagnosis 95 percent of the time."

I brought this advice into my private practice. I made sure that I gave every patient enough time to express what they were feeling. I also gave myself enough time to listen to what they were saying, to diagnose them as best as I could, and to formulate a road map for their wellness.

When I say I leave no stone unturned, it means that I want to hear everything. You need to know that I am listening intently, and that I will address every issue that is brought up.

Hold Nothing Back

Patients come to me from other practitioners, often because they were frustrated with the care that they received. Out of respect for the other doctors, my patients will first try to hold back from telling me why they left that particular doctor. I simply tell them to hold nothing back. This means that when I meet with you, I need to know your expectations as well as your disappointments in your previous healthcare providers, so I can avoid making the same mistakes.

I am pretty confident that my style and approach is different from most conventional doctors, but it's always good to know where the patient is coming from and to assure them that they need not hold anything back.

One of my patients said the other day, "I guess I shouldn't be lying to my own doctor! That will serve me no good."

I assured the patient that, yes, being truthful with me will only get him to his goal and my goal — which is optimal wellness — sooner.

But that all circles back to whether you're comfortable with me, which starts with the first meeting and making sure that there is enough time to build rapport. The doctor-patient relationship is no different from any other and should be an open and honest one.

Tell Me Your Frustrations With the Current Healthcare System

There are a lot of problems with the current healthcare system, as we all know. You are being rushed in and rushed out of a doctor's visit, you are overpaying for your health insurance, and you're not getting the results that you are hoping for. You're feeling pressured to get all your information in front of your doctor in the few minutes you have face-to-face time with them, and ultimately, important pieces of information are left out.

The insurance companies have reduced reimbursement for everything that we do, so in order to keep the profit margin the same as it was before, the logical thing is to increase the volume of patients in a day. The problem, though, is that most doctors don't want to put in longer hours to accommodate that increased volume of patients. So instead of seeing four patients an hour, the doctors have chosen to see six to eight patients in that same hour.

The strains of the healthcare system on physicians have created this chaotic atmosphere in doctors' offices across the country. This needs to stop. Symptoms and issues are being missed, patients are being misdiagnosed, and doctors are dying early from the stress of trying to see all these patients in the allotted time.

The simple solution is to start earlier or stay later or work weekends, which is exactly what I do. Unfortunately, most doctors refuse to sacrifice this personal time. Their patients suffer the consequences — but not my patients. That is why change is needed. The only people affected are the patients.

My mom warned me from day one when I chose to be a doctor that *medicine is the jealous lover.* A jealous lover demands and consumes most of your time, and medicine can be all that. But I have lived by this motto: *Love what you do and do what you love, and you will never work a day in your life.*

I love my job and am good at it. Why? Because I have always been willing to sacrifice the time to get the job done right. Just ask my wife and boys.

This chapter opens with: *Truly listen to your patients, and you will get the diagnosis 95 percent of the time.* That is one of the best pieces of advice I could have ever received for my medical career. I took it to heart. I want you to understand that I *am* listening and creating an atmosphere that will provide the adequate time and environment for you to be heard. It is only when I do this that your diagnosis will become clear to me, 95 percent of the time.

DIVING DEEP

Being a doctor is like being a private detective; we're trying to solve a mystery that involves symptoms. We're trying to find the answer for why you're having all these symptoms. Like any good detective, you can't just scratch the surface with evidence; you have to dive deeper and dig deeper in order to truly get to the root of the problem and solve the mystery.

Getting a Detailed History of the Current Problems

A good practitioner will ask for the details of the story that is being presented. The answers usually lie in those details, so I have to be listening to your story, and I have to actively dig deeper to get those details from you, the patient.

Some patients are easier than others, but the general process requires my prompting you with the right questions in order to create the picture of what's going on. Only this inquiry and truly listening to you will lead to the correct diagnosis.

Sure, I will most likely need laboratory testing, and possibly some imaging, but it all starts with the history.

It all starts with my listening to you and getting that detailed history. It is only then that I can create the correct workup needed in order to get to your diagnosis.

Family History Matters

I have been blessed with three beautiful boys. My oldest son, Tyler, is nineteen years old and just completed his first year of college. He was transferring from one college to another and asked me two weeks ago to do his physical exam in order to enter into his new college.

During his exam, I discovered that he had a cardiac arrhythmia. He is a physically fit, nineteen-year-old soccer player, who absolutely had no symptoms of palpitations, or anything cardiac related. When the workup was finally completed, it turned out that the alcohol he consumed created a toxic environment in his cardiac muscle and thus created this arrhythmia, called *atrial flutter*.

In light of the fact that Tyler is not a very big drinker, he asked me the simple question, "Why?"

There is a cardiac genetic lab test that if positive means that you have a 40 percent chance of having a cardiac event in your life. This could be anything from an arrhythmia all the way up to a heart attack.

When my son asked me why — I knew that his mom was negative, but that I was positive for this cardiac genetic lab test — I looked at him and I said, "I'm willing to bet the twenty bucks in my pocket that you are positive for this lab test because I passed genes down to you. You have a 50/50 chance of having that gene."

The testing for Tyler confirmed that I had passed this down to my son. He will be just fine with proper medication and adjustments in his social habits; however, it is a perfect example of how a family history matters.

Genetics load the gun, but your lifestyle pulls the trigger. In Tyler's case, I passed down this particular gene to him — effectively loading his gun — but his normal weekend intake of alcohol in his freshman year of college pulled the trigger to create this arrhythmia, which we fortunately caught in plenty of time to correct.

It was difficult to believe what I heard when I put the stethoscope on him. Tyler's story illustrates a few important pearls you need to understand. Never underestimate your family history. Your genes play a major role in calculating a potential road map and destination. Your chosen lifestyle determines which route and final destination you reach.

Test, don't guess.

Boston Heart's cardiac gene blood test is available to all doctors, so why isn't your doctor testing you?

Heart disease is the number-one killer in both men and women in the United States.

Wouldn't it be nice to know if you are more at risk than you think?

This piece of knowledge may actually motivate you to change your lifestyle — to be proactive and not reactive. All my patients know if they have this gene.

Shouldn't you?

If you have no system, your lifestyle plan will fail most of the time. I have lost and regained weight my entire life. It was not until I mapped out a system that I met my short-term and long-term goals.

As your coach, mentor, doctor, and friend, I will not only create and implement this system, but keep you on track. I am not afraid to be brutally honest with you and even raise my voice if need be — remember I am Italian and Irish. System = Success!

Now, I have learned my lesson. I'm also constantly learning. Tyler is nineteen, his brother Ryan is seventeen, and Kyle is fifteen. I am going to test them for that gene because knowing about it is information that's crucial, which leads to the next thing: social history.

Social History Is Crucial

Even though Tyler wasn't drinking an excessive amount of alcohol, it was enough for his body to send him into an arrhythmia. If he hadn't switched schools — which forced me to do an exam on him — I never would have caught it because he had just finished his first year of college.

This condition happened only in the last year because he went to college, drank on the weekends, and did the typical college stuff. He was still safe about drinking, but in spite of that, his genetic predisposition simply made him more sensitive to the alcohol. Now that he is aware of this cardiac gene, he will get better.

He asked me if he could ever drink again. I said, "Yes, you can drink, but now you will be aware of when you need to stop, when enough is enough. Your body is going to tell you the threshold at which you need to stop. Your body basically just told us that however many you were drinking up to this point is too much."

He is an adult and will make his own decisions. At least now he is making an informed decision on how to conduct his social life, knowing full well the potential consequences.

I have two other sons, Ryan and Kyle. They too will be tested with this advanced cardiac panel now that they are teenage boys.

I've always taught them that knowledge is power, but I was wrong. Knowledge is potential; *action* is power. The action required will be the lifestyle they choose. They have already been well educated on the dangers of drinking, smoking, drugs, and poor diet, but it will be emphasized even more if they too carry the same gene.

This is the essence of being proactive. My boys and wife are my world. You have your own families and loved ones who depend on you. I cannot prevent what I cannot predict. The workups I perform allow me to accurately predict your course. It is only then that we can formulate a targeted, personalized treatment plan to not just prevent any bad outcomes but achieve optimal wellness.

Another test of the Boston Heart Panel, which is what I've been using for the last ten years, is called *LP(a)*. This, unfortunately, is an *atherogenic* blood test — meaning it increases your risk for plaque — and in this case, by 300 percent.

My maternal grandmother had evidence of congestive heart failure, but no other cardiac history appears in my family. The results of my personal Boston Heart panel show that I am positive for LP(a), as well as the aforementioned cardiac gene. So, I actually have two genes related to possible cardiac issues that were passed down to me.

When I tested myself, I was fifty pounds heavier than I am currently. Doctors feel that they are invincible — we treat diseases, but we think we're never going to get those diseases ourselves. This couldn't be further from the truth. Doing that Boston Heart on myself, I saw all my risk factors, and that moved me off the couch, into the gym, and eating better.

As I said before, genetics load the gun, and lifestyle pulls the trigger. I was going to make sure that my lifestyle wasn't going to pull that trigger. I was going to do everything I could. Anything I can do to change that outcome, I will do, which includes testosterone replacement.

At the time, I had no symptoms of *Low-T*, as they call it. When I learned about the cardio- and neuro-protective effects (most importantly the cardio-protective effects), I wanted that extra layer of protection. For my own personal journey, I decided to get testosterone pellets. That's when I really knew what it was like to have optimal wellness. My energy levels went through the roof, my sleeping became better, and my focus was even sharper than it was before — all with the reassurance that I've given myself the most protection in light of the two genetic factors that I inherited.

I'm just as much of a patient as my patients are. I've learned from my workups, and I have passed this knowledge along to my own patients. Because I can personally relate may be why I have such a good rapport with my patients.

I have been overweight most of my life. I'm Italian and Irish—I love carbohydrates! I love pasta, potatoes, and bread. I am also a former baseball player who dipped tobacco starting at the age of sixteen. I finally stopped that habit ten years ago. I know how hard it is to quit any tobacco products. I can relate to my patients on multiple levels because I've been there.

I've lost weight and gained it back. I understand the commitment it takes to get to the gym on a regular basis. I can explain to them what I have tried, what has worked, what has failed. Through all the trials and errors, I have developed treatment options that work for my patients.

But that's why social history is so crucial, especially when some people may not consider chewing tobacco or dipping tobacco as a risk factor. This goes along with diving deep.

I can't fulfill the wishes of my mom to listen to my patients if I don't have the time to do it. The current healthcare system is a mess, and it doesn't allow me to have that time to truly listen to my patients, which could lead to misdiagnosis.

The change that needed to take place was for me to break away from the traditional medical practice and create concierge-type medicine that allows me all the time to listen to my patients, to dig deep, to go through the crucial family and social histories, and to build rapport so they feel comfortable. Just like any good detective, a good doctor is one who will listen and take all factors into consideration in order to solve the mystery. Once the mystery is solved, I formulate a treatment plan.

CHAPTER THREE

———————————

My Journey

No man is a good doctor who has never been sick himself.
~ Chinese Proverb

HOLIDAY HEART

My own journey as a patient started during the holiday season in 2007. It was at that moment that I realized that even though I preached good health, *I* wasn't in good health at all. I tell you about my personal journey to help you better understand where I am coming from and the reason why I am writing this book.

Palpitations

On Christmas Day 2007, I was enjoying my time off; I was watching a Christmas show with my son Tyler. I felt a palpitation, or a flickering of my heart, for the first time in my life. At first, I ignored the symptom, but then I decided to check my pulse to see if it correlated with an actual irregular heartbeat. At that moment, I felt my pulse skip a beat, then pause, then go back into a normal rhythm, accompanied with a fluttering in my throat that radiated up to my jaw.

I then recalled that a few of my colleagues had passed away within the past year from sudden heart attacks.

My thought was: *Oh my God, I do not want to be one of those doctors they'll be reading about in the paper!*

It was out of this fear to not become a statistic that I decided to put my health in the care of a cardiologist.

The medical world is an interesting world in which we're in complete denial over our own health. As I sat on the couch in my living room, with my three young boys running around me, I knew that I had to dig deeper — if not for my sake, then for the sake of my family.

I Became the Patient

Calling my cardiology colleague and going over the symptoms, it was decided that I needed a cardiac stress test. For some reason, I became the patient with the attitude that the test would reveal the holiday experience was just a fluke.

So, there I was, in my buddy the cardiologist's office, in my workout gear on a treadmill. Five minutes into the stress test, the nurse quietly leaned over and whispered something into the cardiologist's ear. I don't think she realized that I was a physician and was familiar with stress testing, but I also saw the EKG changes that were happening right before my eyes as I was running on the treadmill. I also noted that my blood pressure was 200/105 at peak exercise.

When the stress test was over, my cardiologist felt that further testing was needed. I distinctly remember driving home in tears because after all these years of studying and working, I was convinced that I now had heart disease, putting me at increased risk for a fatal heart attack.

Earning an MD Degree Does Not Make You Infallible

Luckily, my nuclear stress test confirmed that the exercise stress test was indeed a false alarm. However, the elevated blood pressure was real, and so was my obesity at the time. One of the possibilities for my initial blood pressure being so high, and the false alarm with the stress test, may have been sleep apnea. I have three home sleep apnea units in my office. Not once had I ever put one on myself.

On my way home from the cardiologist's office, I stopped by my office to pick up a unit so I could apply it to myself that night. This resulted in the discovery that I indeed had sleep apnea, more pronounced when I lay on my back. As it turned out, the sleep apnea was from a severe deviated septum injury from my high school football days, and I quickly got it corrected with surgery.

Becoming a patient was a very profound experience in my life. I realized that I am not infallible. I realized that I needed to make time out of my incredibly busy schedule to remain healthy for my family. In retrospect, becoming a patient was the best thing that ever happened in my life.

I experienced the fear of potential death. I experienced feelings of *Oh my, look what happened due to my unhealthy lifestyle!* I had given myself every reason not to go to the gym, and I had rationalized my way through all the nachos with melted cheese that my boys loved to eat with me, as well as the popcorn drizzled with butter at the movies, and all the other snacks that I shared with my young boys.

The palpitations turned out to be a gift that Christmas. It opened my eyes to what I needed to do and what I needed to change in my life. I needed to practice what I preached.

OVERWEIGHT

Obesity is an epidemic in our country. I have battled my weight my entire life. I know what it's like to try to hide the gut, and I know how hard it is to lose weight.

The Husky Section of J. C. Penney

Every August during my elementary school years, I hopped in the car with mom to go get my school clothes for the year. I vividly remember walking into the J. C. Penney store and going straight to the husky section. It was tucked away in the corner of the store, where all the other overweight kids were trying on clothes. It was natural for me because those were the only clothes that fit me at the time, and because I had never shopped for my school clothes in the regular section of the store.

Another story that I will always remember was during a Vermont trip with the family when I was ten years old. I was a huge *Happy Days* fan, and Fonzie was my favorite character growing up. I was wearing a T-shirt with a picture of Fonzie on the front.

When I walked into the church on a Sunday morning, the priest stopped me and said, "It looks like Fonzie has a lot of gas!"

I laughed because everybody else did, but I realized that the priest was actually commenting on how tight my T-shirt was over my obese belly.

Nearly forty years later I still remember that day like it was yesterday. I still remember the sights and the smells of the husky section of J. C. Penney.

The point I'm trying to make is that I, too, am part of the obesity epidemic in the United States. I know what it feels like to be overweight. I understand the embarrassment and the frustration of being overweight.

The Carbohydrate Addict's Healthy Heart Diet

I married my high school sweetheart, Janice, the summer after I graduated medical school. We were married before I started my intern year, so we postponed our honeymoon until my winter break, six months later. Even though we had been together since we were sixteen years old, I had never gone grocery shopping with her. Apparently, my first duty as a husband was to join her at the local Stop & Shop.

I begrudgingly agreed to go because we were newly-weds, but the minute we entered, I immediately took a sharp left toward the book section. My plan was to see if there were any sports magazines that would entertain me and keep me from shopping—something I have dreaded my entire life.

I came across a paperback book called *The Carbohydrate Addict's Healthy Heart Diet*. The title drew my attention because I knew how addicted I was to carbohydrates. I started to read it in the middle of Stop & Shop, not necessarily to avoid shopping with Janice, but because it piqued my interest, and I could not put the book down.

After twenty years of studying, the last thing I wanted to do was add more reading material to my daily activities, but this book just drew me in. I bought it, I read it, and I followed it religiously. The book taught me how to eat. Even as a new doctor, the book taught me the difference between a good carbohydrate and a bad carbohydrate. It was the guide that catapulted me into at least the start of a healthy lifestyle.

The key point here is that while I lost weight by following the guidelines in that book when I was first married, the stories of snacking with my sons clearly show that I gained it all back twelve years later. That was when I became a patient. In spite of knowing how to eat for optimum health, at that time and for whatever reason, I chose not to maintain that way of eating for the rest of my life.

Ideal Protein

My mom was an avid reader of medical journals and of nontraditional medical literature. She was a big fan of Dr. Robert Atkins and his approach to dieting and controlling blood sugar and insulin. I was never a good listener, not even with one of the best teachers I could have ever had in my life.

However, I do remember — during college years when I was playing baseball at Yale University — my mother putting me on a MEVY diet:

- Meat
- Eggs
- Vegetables
- Yogurt

She created it herself, based on her readings within her library of medical literature from naturopathic doctors, homeopathic doctors, and nontraditional doctors who understood the insulin and sugar relationship.

The MEVY diet was given to me after my freshman year, and it worked wonderfully. Unfortunately, it worked so well, and I lost so much weight that by the time I started up my sophomore year with baseball, I could not hit a ball out of the infield. I needed to take up weightlifting in order to regain the power that I had when I was overweight.

Twenty-three years later, I discovered the *Ideal Protein* program. In 2015, it was voted the number-one diet in the world. It is basically a low-carb, high-protein diet that focuses on foods such as meat, eggs, vegetables, and yogurt. After reviewing this diet, I quickly realized the accuracy of the diet my mom created for me in 1987 after my freshman year in college. She was twenty-eight years ahead of her time.

Being overweight has a profound impact on your outlook, your confidence, and your psyche in general. You get used to wearing the oversized shirt and pants to hide the extra pounds. I am all too familiar with this scenario.

PRACTICE WHAT I PREACH

I feel that the success of my practice has been the mere fact that I can relate to all my patients at one level or another. The most prominent problems that I can relate to are my patients' struggles with their weight, dieting, and changing their lifestyle.

I Am a Yo-Yo Too

Unfortunately, the term *yo-yo diet* is very apt. The bad thing about yo-yo dieting is that when you lose the initial twenty or thirty pounds, you are losing a combination of muscle and fat, and a little bit of water weight. However, when you regain that twenty or thirty pounds, you're regaining it all in fat — no muscle at all.

I have been a yo-yo dieter my entire life. The pictures that I have throughout my adult life show the skinny days, as well as the obese days. Even after my event with the palpitations and my false-alarm stress test, I initially lost the weight that I needed to lose, but then eventually gained it all back. It wasn't until my boys were older that I realized there was a much greater purpose for me to lose the weight and get healthy.

Nobody Wants Advice From a Fat Doctor

It's really simple. I know that you don't want me talking about how to diet, exercise, and lose weight when I'm overweight myself as I advise you. I realized that I lose all credibility, in spite of all my studying and my research, if I don't practice what I preach.

My mother told me clearly in her loving, Italian way, "Kevin, nobody wants advice from a fat doctor."

Once again, she was correct in her assessment. So, I made a commitment to get myself into shape and create a different lifestyle for myself. My motivations were my family and my patients.

My ultimate dream was to become a doctor and help others. I needed to exemplify what I was trying to get across to my patients, but more importantly, I needed to be alive so I could spread the word to all these potential patients who needed my help. I needed to stay alive for my family that means everything to me.

Staying on Track Is Hard

Four years ago—when I finally decided to reinvent myself and change my entire lifestyle with regards to how I eat, exercise, and approach life in general—I lost fifty pounds and then decided to get back in the gym. It was a slow but determined journey to reshape my body and create an image that I was proud of.

However, once you get to that end point, it's difficult to stay on track.

You feel great about yourself, and you think: *You know what? I can have that piece of bread with butter on it because I'm fifty pounds lighter now.*

During a physical exam for a renewed life insurance policy, I was asked how much I weigh. Once I lost the weight, I never stepped on a scale again. This is because my clothes always fit fine, and I didn't want to be married to the scale. I estimated that I was 200 pounds, but when I was told my weight was actually 222 pounds, my heart sunk into my stomach.

It became clear to me that maintaining my weight needed to be something I did on a daily basis, and that I needed to stay on track. I did not want to lose everything that I had worked so hard for in the three to four years prior. I regrouped, got back into the gym, and restarted my journey once again.

You should understand that staying on track can be difficult. When you work with me, I am not only your doctor; I am your coach. By telling you my own stories, you understand that I know exactly what you're going through. I remind myself every day to stay on track, and that's what you need to do as well.

To have credibility and gain your confidence and trust, I need to show you the result of this treatment program that I am laying out for you. It has never come easily in my life to stay physically fit. You need a plan. Without a plan, you are going to fail. I want to create that plan. I want to create that motivation. I want to stay on top of my patients so they stay on track. Again, I need to practice what I preach, like every good coach should.

I share the stories with my patients in my exam rooms. It opens up dialogue. Some of my patients have been with me for twenty years, and they have seen the ups and downs.

I have introduced weight lifting into my program, and recently one of my patients congratulated me.

"Wow, Doc, you're keeping the weight off and you look great!"

I reminded them that it's a daily grind.

With my schedule the way it is now, in order to maintain that daily grind, I have to get up at 4:30 every morning, which is not a big deal as long as I go to bed at 9:30 every night. *That's* where the challenge is because my kids play sports, and there are many activities we are involved with in the evenings. As long as I'm disciplined at night, then I can get up at 4:30.

For me, I need to get my workout in before my day starts because once the day starts, forget it. But it's that important in my life, and I try to explain that to my patients. Invest the time; you are so worth it.

CHAPTER FOUR

The Forever Student

Medicine is the jealous lover.
~ Shirley Greene, RN

MEDICINE IS NOT A BUSINESS

Doctors are notorious for not being good businessmen and businesswomen. I'm the first to admit that. When I started my private practice, I hired my brother, Jack, who has his MBA from Cornell University, to guide me. I was smart enough to hand the business side over to my brother, while I focused on the clinical side and taking care of my patients.

The biggest challenge for physicians who decide to go into practice is to realize that although their practice is a business, providing private medical care is actually an art. It's what we train for and study for our entire lives, and it's up to us to draw that line between the business side and the compassionate, medical side of things.

Remember the Hippocratic Oath

When I completed my residency at the University of Connecticut Medical Center, I was given a unique opportunity to hang my shingle, if you will, in the town of Southington, Connecticut. At the time, the hospital was recruiting doctors to take on new patients in exchange for the startup cost for the practice. It was a perfect marriage. I grew up in the next town over, in Wolcott, Connecticut, and had always wanted to practice in Southington.

When starting a private practice, it is essentially a business. It is a double-edged sword. One could focus on the business side of things and lose the personal and humanistic side of being a doctor or alternatively, focus on the medical side of things and run the business into the ground. I never claimed to be a businessman; I was trained to be a doctor.

Overhead, expenses, and other costs are associated with starting a medical practice, so I couldn't forget that my practice was a business as well. Luckily, my greatest mentor—my mom—was constantly reminding me of the fact that I was there as a doctor, not as a businessman.

The first line of the Hippocratic oath is interpreted as: *Do no harm.*

It is tricky and challenging to remain a compassionate, caring doctor while trying to run a private practice. I had the good fortune of having an MBA in my oldest brother, and an incredible nurse as my mother. So, as my brother watched the business side of things, my mom was constantly reminding me to remain myself and never lose sight of the reason I chose my profession.

If I'd Wanted to Be a Millionaire, I Would Have Worked on Wall Street

I had the privilege of being accepted into Yale University after graduating from my public high school in Wolcott. It was an honor to be representing my town for the first time at such a prestigious university. I had the pleasure of meeting some of my best friends in the world, as well as some of the most amazing minds with regards to business. I started college intending to become an electrical engineer; my plans were to own IBM.

However, during my sophomore year, when I took my first electrical engineering class, I realized it was not the profession I wanted to go into. I was distraught at the time because my entire focus had been on becoming an electrical engineer. I realized that it wasn't a field I loved.

Shortly after, I started volunteering at Yale New Haven Hospital and explored the world of medicine. That is where my love for medicine began—particularly in the Wound Care Center. The Center took care of New Haven-area victims of horrific burns; in my eyes, it was a world of exploration and helping others who were in such great need and such great pain.

I wanted more, and more, and more. Luckily, my electrical engineering classes also qualified as pre-med classes, so I didn't lose much ground by switching to pre-med.

After years of studying medicine, I found it interesting to get an email from one of my fraternity brothers who worked on Wall Street. Four years of college, followed by medical school, I was an intern at the University of Connecticut Health Center, working thirty-six hour shifts every three days. I was making $36,000 a year and working over one hundred hours a week. Don't get me wrong; I loved every minute of it because this was what I wanted to do.

However, that email from my Wall Street fraternity brother spoke of celebrating their year-end bonus of $200,000. I laughed and reminded myself that this is the profession that I chose to go into, and that if I wanted to be a millionaire, I would be right next to my buddy on Wall Street. That email confirmed for me my passion and my dedication to the world of medicine; I knew my place in the world, and the money didn't really matter at that point.

Love what you do and do what you love is something that I have always professed to my three boys. I've always told them that nothing is worse than waking up every day and going to a job that you don't like or love. I love my job. I'm fortunate to wake up every day to do work that I love.

I actually graduated with a chemical engineering degree. I got a lot of strange looks when I was going through my medical school interviews. One of the doctors asked me if I was lost.

I laughed and said, "No, I love chemical engineering, but I love medicine more. So, I'm not lost."

Board Certification for Mom and My Patients

Since the day I entered medical school, my mom always told me that board certification status is the first thing that she looks for in a doctor. In her mind, it set the standard for excellence in whatever field that doctor chose. So, after medical school and my residency training, I became board certified. The board certification only lasted ten years.

At the ten-year mark, I had a busy practice, and my patients knew exactly what they were getting with me as their doctor. It didn't affect me financially, meaning that the insurance companies did not care whether I was board certified or not. Like I said, at that point in my career, I was as busy as I wanted to be.

When my mom asked me why I let my board certification lapse, I explained to her that I really didn't have time to study for the board exam because I was running a business. I actually put it in those exact words. My mom looked at me with disappointment across her face, and reminded me, once again, that medicine is not a business.

She held that board certification to heart and was proud of the fact that her son was a board-certified physician. It didn't matter to her whether I had time to study, or how it affected the bottom line of the private practice. She knew that it wasn't going to increase my income at all to be board certified; what was important was the actual certification.

In her mind, board certification represented my commitment to my patients and to myself — to maintain a level of excellence in my field of medicine. Because of that, I decided to retake the boards, which I then passed, not for business, but for my mom and for my patients.

I've always been open to any and all criticism of my office, my staff, and my approach with the patients. I rarely paid attention to any of the social media opinions of me, but one particularly stuck in my mind: a patient described me as a person who was more interested in the business than in being a doctor.

That one cut deep because it made me realize that I had failed this particular patient. He had a wrong impression of who I am, but his opinion was justified. It was a very powerful wakeup call for me to take another look at the way I was practicing medicine in private practice and go back to my roots of being a doctor first, and the owner of the practice second.

KNOWLEDGE IS POWER

School always came first in the Greene household. I had a love for sports, but it was clear that sports were second after my schoolwork was done. It became a challenge to me, through my years of school, that not only did I want to be the best in the classroom, I wanted to excel on the ball field. I soon realized that the knowledge that I was gathering and the report cards that I was earning built my confidence and molded me into the person that I am now.

I had a thirst for knowledge throughout my entire schooling, starting from Ms. Mathews' classroom in first grade, to Mr. DelCioppo in middle school, all the way to Mr. Desjarlais, my beloved calculus teacher at Wolcott High School.

One concept I try to model for my three kids is that knowledge is power. I was proud to see that my first son, Tyler's, school project in fourth grade was a poster of Darth Vader with the title, *Knowledge Is Power*. One of my proudest moments was realizing that what I was saying to my boys was getting through to them.

Medicine Is Constantly Changing

The world of medicine is constantly in a state of flux. What was determined to be safe years ago has now been determined to be unsafe, due to the advances in science that we are making every day. Medicine is discovering new treatment modalities, new diagnostic equipment, and is everchanging.

I was trained in an era of exciting changes in the medical world. HIV and AIDS hit the mainstream in my last year of college, and that field alone showed incredible growth and advancement throughout my medical school career, as well as during my residency training. It is amazing to me that HIV is now considered a chronic disease, not a death sentence. While training on the HIV unit at Hartford Hospital, we were losing patients on a daily basis to this deadly virus. That is just one example of how medicine is constantly changing.

It is my duty as your doctor to stay on top of all these changes. I have discovered that I have an incredible interest in the cardiovascular side of medicine, but I went into internal medicine for one reason: I want to treat the entire patient as a whole. I didn't want to become a cardiologist just to deal with the heart. I didn't want to become an orthopedic surgeon just to deal with broken bones. I want to be ready for any patient who walks into my waiting room.

It Needs to Be Evidence-Based

After my journey at Yale University, I had the privilege of being accepted into Georgetown University School of Medicine. It was an incredible learning experience while living in the nation's capital. Of all the things I learned in my medical school career, one of the best classes I have ever taken was a class that taught us how to interpret a study.

This class went into details on what a *P Value* meant and the sensitivity and specificity of a particular study. The class was powerful to me because it gave me the knowledge to distinguish which studies were clearly evidence-based, not biased by a pharmaceutical company or special interest group.

When I study about the advances and all the new discoveries in medicine, I always go back to that one class to make sure that the study that I am reading about is real, true, and accurate. Everything I do in my office is evidence-based. This assures my patients that there have been studies that have been conducted that prove the validity of the tests or treatment regimens that I recommend.

Too many doctors rely on studies that are not evidence-based. This is real and should be a major concern for all patients.

Staying on the Cutting Edge

One of my first patients in Southington, Connecticut, was a forty-five-year-old female patient who was suffering from diabetes. When she came into my office, her sugar was extremely high, at 245.

When asked if these were her usual sugars with her old physician, she looked at me in confusion and said, "Yeah, these have always been my sugars. My doctor, in fact, said that he likes his patients to be a little on the sweet side."

Her doctor had a good reputation in the community and took good care of many patients. However, he was not on the cutting edge of diabetes management.

Multiple studies have shown that you need to be aggressive with diabetes management, even if it means causing the sugars to go low. The studies also determined that there are microvascular changes that take place in a patient with diabetes whose sugar levels remain high.

My patient soon discovered how aggressive she needed to be with her diabetes management. This included a better diet, a better exercise regimen, a much tighter control of her sugar throughout her day, and extensive education on what she should do to keep her sugars in the normal range, which was our goal. I also warned her that my goals were a little stricter than some of the national guidelines, and that as her doctor, I was also going to be her coach.

The reason why I am so aggressive with my patients' treatment plans, especially for patients with diabetes, is that evidence-based medicine has shown that with tighter control, even at the expense of lower blood sugars, patients are going to live longer and experience less cardiovascular complications down the road.

Prevention is the key to an effective treatment plan. I would rather be proactive and not reactive. Patients need to buy into the fact that even if there are no signs of illness now, continuing on their current path will likely result in health challenges. That's why the treatment plan needs to be aggressive, and patients need to be willing to stay the course. When they do, they will be rewarded with optimal health.

I am a firm believer in continuing education. If I had not attended conferences over the past ten years, I would not be writing this book! It was at these conferences that I learned of all the new advances in medicine. They led me to explore conferences on anti-aging, functional medicine, and thinking outside the box of standard medical care.

I will continue to dedicate time for education. Education has defined me since I entered first grade. My mom strove to impress this on me, and she taught me from day one the importance of self-education and the power that knowledge can hold.

YOU DESERVE THE BEST

In the world of accounting, if you make a mistake, somebody loses money. In the world of medicine, mistakes can lead to harm, if not death. I am saddened by the state of the medical field today; vital information and crucial follow-up have fallen through the cracks.

Since I'm your physician, you trust me. Just as I excelled in the classrooms of Wolcott, Connecticut, and Yale University, and on the ball fields of Waterbury, Connecticut, I need to be the best for my patients and in my field of medicine.

Deal #1: You Trust Me; I Keep Studying

Trust is a powerful word and one that I take seriously. If you are entrusting me with your health, then I have an obligation to study. It's really that simple.

As I said earlier, I knew going into this profession that *medicine is a jealous lover*. My mom's advice to me rang loud and clear the minute I started having children. I have not gone to every baseball game, soccer game, or school event with my three boys. I've missed many family moments because of the profession that I chose. I don't regret any of that, but you need to know that's how seriously I take my job. If you are going to trust me with your health, my end of the bargain is to keep studying so I can be at the top of my profession.

Deal #2: I Stay Healthy for You

I need to practice what I preach. There have been multiple times in my life when I have been overweight and morbidly obese. I've used the excuse that I'm too busy studying to work out and eat a healthy diet, but I realize that if I preach good health, I need to represent good health.

It is not easy. I wake up every morning at 4:30 so I can get in an hour-and-a-half workout before my day starts at 7:00. I'm not merely in the office at 7:00, I am seeing patients at 7:00. This has been my custom throughout my career; patients need to get to work, and the only time that I can fit them in and remain healthy is first thing in the morning. It is not easy and requires discipline to stay true to my health, but it is my promise to you.

I made this commitment for my patients and for my family. I realize the need to represent good health, but I also need to stay healthy for my patients. What good am I if I need to deal with my own preventable illnesses?

Deal #3: I Never Forget Why I Became a Doctor

As my career has evolved over the last ten years, I realized that I needed to go back to my roots. This means I need to go back to being my patients' doctor, not the owner of my practice. I delegated many of my responsibilities to trustworthy people so I can concentrate on being the doctor in my practice.

One of my favorite poems defines what it is to be a success. I realize that success is not measured by how much money is in my bank account, but how I affect the lives of other people. I appreciate my job and love being a doctor.

To Laugh Often and Much

To laugh often and much;
to win the respect of the intelligent people
and the affection of children;
to earn the appreciation of honest critics
and endure the betrayal of false friends;
to appreciate beauty;
to find the best in others;
to leave the world a bit better
whether by a healthy child, a garden patch,
or a redeemed social condition;
to know that one life has breathed easier
because you lived here.
This is to have succeeded.
~ often attributed to Emerson

I try to live by this poem. Being a doctor is a privilege; I realize that. Being a father and a husband is a privilege, and I realize that. These are the words that guide me through my life, and I have learned to appreciate every step of my journey. It has not been an easy journey, but it is my journey. It has led me to writing this book, and I hope it will lead me to taking care of you and making you breathe a little bit easier in your life. This is why I became a doctor. And yes, Mom, I am finally listening to your words.

I never claimed to know everything in my field. But if I don't know something, you can rest assured that I will be studying the latest research that evening. All personal plans will be put aside for me to become knowledgeable about the condition. This is how I was raised, and this is who I am.

You deserve to have the best healthcare provider — someone who:

- Listens to you
- Is open to your feedback
- Coaches you
- Works hard to educate self and patients

This is what you deserve.

CHAPTER FIVE

Seven Pillars of Optimal Wellness

It always seems impossible until it is done.
~ Nelson Mandela

THE SEVEN PILLARS

The seven pillars of optimal wellness serve as a metaphor for considering the whole person—body, mind, and soul—when addressing health needs. You may find them worded differently or even trademarked by other physicians.

I consider the seven major pillars to be:

1. Diet
2. Exercise
3. Detox
4. Supplements
5. Hormones

6. Brainwaves
7. NAD

Carbs Kill

It's very simple — carbs kill. Being Italian and Irish, I love my pasta, bread, and potatoes too. However, it is now well known that a low-carbohydrate diet is far superior than a low-fat diet.

It's not the carbohydrates that do the damage, it is the insulin that is released in response to the carbohydrates that does all the damage. Insulin is a vital hormone that plays a major role in our sugar balance. However, when we have too much of it, insulin stores fat and is a major contributor to the metabolic syndrome.

The metabolic syndrome is a condition of excess insulin that can lead to elevated cholesterol, increased belly fat, diabetes, and heart disease.

The simple solution is to avoid carbohydrates, right?

Yeah right!

Easier said than done. I don't need a study to tell me this; I battle it personally every day. This concept of a low-carb diet is the foundation for the Atkins diet, South Beach diet, Ideal Protein system, and now even the Weight Watchers system. To be successful with this lifestyle change, I'm convinced that you need a practical system, a motivated coach, and tons of encouragement.

Diet is the first and most important pillar of all the seven. It is a crucial step for optimal health and wellness. This is where true teamwork needs to be applied. Like a domino effect, a low-carb, high-protein diet creates the foundation in which to build on all the other pillars. This requires true education on the effects of food and water on your health and a lot of faith that diet program we tailored for you will work. No worries—it will.

Lift Weights

Muscle burns fat. It's a simple rule and fact to live by. If you have thirty minutes to either go for a walk, a run, or do some sort of resistance exercise—whether it's with resistance bands or free weights—I am going to advise you to exercise with the resistance bands and free weights. The reason is that your return on investment will be much greater with this choice.

Think of muscle as a furnace, burning away at the fat, even when you're sitting down. Once again: *muscle burns fat*. The key is to get lean and put muscle on your body.

In January 2017, my dream of attaching a full-strength academy to my internal medicine practice came true. Once a week, approximately 150 of my beloved patients come to my gym and go through a thirty-minute lesson on how to properly lift weights for that particular week. With this approach, patients avoid injuries, they build muscle, and their subsequent lab work shows incredible improvements.

Patients love coming here and working out because they feel better on the inside, and they look better on the outside. By the way, the age range of the patients who come to my full-strength academy is from nineteen to ninety-two years old.

The Liver Is Boss

A lot of doctors tend to forget that the liver needs to be detoxed to accept all these changes. Whether it's food, supplements, or medications, it all goes through the liver for the detoxification process. In order for vitamins to properly work in our bodies, we need to not only absorb them in our gut, but we need to make sure that they survive the liver. The liver is definitely the boss when trying to achieve optimal health and results.

SUPPLEMENTS AND HORMONES

Not all of us have the perfect diet that gives us the proper dosage of vitamins that the body needs to achieve optimal health. Therefore, we need to reach out and find the right vitamins from the right company in order to get the best results. Hormones are also vital for cardio protection and optimal health. There are many myths regarding vitamins and hormones, and I'm here to set the story straight.

You Get What You Pay For

Forty to fifty years ago, the FDA declared that vitamins were no longer considered a food. With this declaration, the watchdog organization walked away from vitamin companies. Unfortunately, this meant that a lot of the nutraceutical companies decided to cut corners with the fillers that they put in each of their vitamins, which became dangerous to patients.

Through the years, new watchdogs have formed to ensure that nutraceutical companies are following certain rules and regulations to produce safe products. Xymogen is the company that I have chosen to use for my supplements because it is an honest company that has passed all the proper regulations and tests in order to become a top nutraceutical company.

When I'm going over results with my patients, I pull out a Xymogen order sheet and tell them the supplements that I feel are needed based on their abnormal labs. The patients will then take that supplement sheet and go to the nearest Walmart or Costco and get the less expensive alternatives.

It is only six months later, when we repeat the blood work that we see that none of the results have changed. This illustrates the importance of having your vitamins be absorbed in order for them to do their work. I try to explain to patients that the reason Xymogen products are more expensive is because there is much more research that goes into achieving the ultimate absorption of the vitamins for optimal results.

I tell patients that they may have saved money each month by buying the cheaper alternatives; however, they sacrificed their health and their goals weren't achieved. They, in essence, got what they paid for.

Don't Underestimate the Thyroid

The thyroid hormone hits every organ in the entire body. It is one of the most vital organs. However, it wasn't until a few years ago that I realized I was taught incorrectly how to monitor the thyroid. We were taught to use a lab test for TSH, which is secreted by the adrenal gland. So, in essence, we are asking the adrenal gland to tell us what it thinks about the thyroid gland, which is in a different part of the body, to put it simply.

When your thyroid makes a hormone, it makes something called T4. However, T4 is completely inert and does not have any effect on our bodies. T4, then, needs to be converted to T3, and from there, the T3 needs to be unbound from a protein that attaches to it, creating Free T3. The Free T3 is the workhorse of the thyroid. It produces most, if not all, of the effects of the thyroid gland.

However, doctors rarely check the Free T3 because we were never taught about it. When I started checking the Free T3 levels, I now had a reason for those patients who had been complaining about not feeling well on their thyroid medications.

These patients were all being treated with a medicine that replaced the T4, when in fact what they needed replenished was the Free T3, which is a completely different medication. The thyroid should never be underestimated and should be looked at closely, especially the Free T3 level.

Testosterone!

Four years ago, I went to Dallas, Texas, to learn all about testosterone through a company called BioTE. It was the most informative and incredible lecture series I've ever had in my career up to that point. Not once were erection and libido mentioned over the course of two days. The purpose of the lecture was to teach doctors how testosterone protects the heart, first and foremost, the brain second, and has properties to protect us from cancer. Additionally, testosterone is the best way to increase our bone strength.

The organ that has the most testosterone receptors is the heart. Here I am, considering myself a well-read doctor on the subject of cardiovascular prevention, and I don't even realize that testosterone is cardio-protective for patients.

Testosterone has incredible properties. Testosterone not only protects the heart, the brain, and bones, but also helps build muscle, which will then burn fat, as mentioned previously. If I'm truly going to be a proactive physician for you, and I want to protect you from heart disease the number one killer in America, then testosterone must be mentioned in the conversation.

Another factor when measuring testosterone levels is that normal levels, according to lab results, are not necessarily the optimal levels. We need to be aggressive in our hormone replacement therapy if we are going to properly protect the heart and the patient from cardiovascular disease and death.

These are two of my most favorite pillars to talk about with my patients. There is such confusion over which supplements are the right ones to take and many myths about the dangers of hormone therapy. There is no danger in hormone therapy, as long as the physician is aware of how to test for them, and how to treat them in a safe manner.

When advanced cardiovascular testing is done, it's possible to target the supplements that need to be replaced. I call this *targeted therapy,* so there's no waste of money and we're taking the minimum number of vitamins needed to achieve optimal health.

When you replace the hormones properly, under the right guidance of the doctor, not only are the patients protected, but they feel fantastic. They sleep better, their energy goes through the roof, they have an excellent outlook on life, and their libidos are elevated as well. It's a win-win situation when you properly replace the supplements and hormones.

BRAINWAVES

The brain has four categories of brainwaves:

1. Delta
2. Theta
3. Alpha
4. Beta

They each have their own specific role when dealing with the outside world and certain situations. When these brainwaves are not regulated, we need to correct this dis-regulation. It is vital for the patient to understand the essential role of brainwaves and how crucial it is to have regulation and balance.

I invested in a system called *Braincore,* which allows me to do a brain map. The brain map diagnoses which brainwaves are dis-regulated. Based on these results, treatment protocols are then generated that use a system called *neurofeedback.* In the past, this type of work up and treatment was only offered in a research laboratory. I offer all this in the comfort of my office. And the best news is that once all your brainwaves are regulated, it is permanent.

Brain mapping and neurofeedback have been studied for forty years and have a major impact on our health. If I am treating you as a whole person, this vital function simply cannot be ignored.

Have you ever been brain mapped?

I'm willing to guess most of you have not.

NAD

NAD is the closest we've gotten to a fountain of youth. It's one of the most important molecules for life to exist, and without it, you're dead in thirty seconds.
~ David Sinclair, Co-Director
Paul F. Glenn Center for the Biology of Aging
Harvard Medical School

NAD stands for *nicotinamide adenine dinucleotide*. NAD is a coenzyme molecule that creates cellular energy and helps maintain the body's metabolism. NAD is created naturally in every cell in the body as an essential enzyme that produces cellular energy. NAD provides the bio-fuel for every cell and organ in the body.

NAD was first discovered in 1936, but World War II stopped the research. It was patented for treatment of drug addiction and schizophrenia in 1961 based on an eleven thousand-patient study. Sloughed aside with the discovery of methadone—a far more lucrative choice at the time for drug companies—NAD went *underground.*

Studies have found that those with extremely low NAD levels are far more vulnerable to addiction as well as other chronic diseases. There is a preponderance of low levels of NAD present in Western society as it is mostly lost in cooking and food processing. What little remains is broken down by stomach acid, degraded before it's absorbed from the digestive tract.

When all-natural NAD is received directly through an IV, the nutrients bypass the stomach and go directly to the receptors in the brain and throughout the body. At Optimal Wellness, I administer the life-restorative compound directly into your blood circulation, optimizing the potential for absorbing this life-enhancing nutrient. Five days of consecutive IV therapy with NAD is delivered in a tailored approach to meet your individual needs.

There is a direct link between health and energy production. NAD is responsible for health and energy at a cellular level. Compelling research has shown that when supplementing with IV NAD, individuals are affectively recovering from the following medical conditions:

- Chronic fatigue syndrome
- Depression
- Neurodegenerative diseases
- Acute anxiety disorders
- Post-traumatic stress
- Cognitive impairment
- Chronic traumatic encephalopathy (CTE)
- Chronic stress
- Chemo brain
- Anti-aging
- Autoimmune diseases
- Chronic pain
- Addictions

Both poor lifestyle and aging deplete our bodies of this miracle molecule. I will give NAD back to you intravenously and then modify your lifestyle. You will live longer and truly experience optimal health.

This treatment is another example of how I deliver scientifically-proven, cutting-edge research to the patient rooms of Optimal Wellness Center.

Conclusion

Invest in your health. You and the ones you love are worth it. I don't treat patients; I educate them and empower them to take care of themselves. We become a team. It takes teamwork to make a dream work. If we remain positive and proactive, then the sky is the limit. Always remember that attitude determines altitude. Your outlook will determine your outcome.

Reclaim your health, your youth, and your life.

Knowledge is potential; action is power!

Make the call.

Reclaim your beautiful life.

Next Steps

Be sure to visit our website, LiveOptimalWellness.com, and like us on Facebook at Optimal Wellness Center, facebook.com/DrKevinPGreene/.

For more information on optimal health, give our office a call for an appointment today at 203-584-5900.

Let us help guide you on your search for optimal wellness.

About the Author

Kevin P. Greene, MD, graduated from Yale University in 1990 with a BA in Chemical Engineering. He then went to medical school and graduated from Georgetown University School of Medicine in 1995.

Dr. Greene completed his Internal Medicine Residency Program at the University of Connecticut, and he earned Intern of the Year in 1996.

More recently, he was named the Best Doctor of Southington, 2002.

Dr. Greene's health optimization approach combines the best of all evidence-based medicine to give his patients a wider range of choices. This approach embodies elements from traditional, integrative, functional, and age-management medicine; and he employs them in a preventive, proactive way to meet each patient's specific needs.

Dr. Greene's goal for every patient is for them to achieve optimal wellness.